CUBA 2016 HUMAN RIGHTS REPORT

EXECUTIVE SUMMARY

Cuba is an authoritarian state led by Raul Castro, who is president of the Council of State and Council of Ministers, Communist Party (CP) first secretary, and commander in chief of security forces. The constitution recognizes the CP as the only legal party and the leading force of society and of the state. The government conducted the April 2015 municipal elections with relative administrative efficiency, but they were neither free nor fair; a CP candidacy commission prescreened all candidates and the government treated non-CP candidates differently.

The national leadership, including members of the military, maintained effective control over the security forces.

The principal human rights abuses included the abridgement of the ability of citizens to choose their government; the use of government threats, physical assault, intimidation, and violent government-organized counter protests against peaceful dissent; and harassment and detentions to prevent free expression and peaceful assembly.

The following additional abuses continued: harsh prison conditions; arbitrary, short-term, politically motivated detentions and arrests; selective prosecution; denial of fair trial; and travel restrictions. Authorities interfered with privacy by engaging in significant monitoring and censoring of private communications. The government did not respect freedoms of speech and press, restricted internet access, maintained a monopoly on media outlets, circumscribed academic freedom, and maintained some restrictions on the ability of unregistered religious groups to gather. The government refused to recognize independent human rights groups or permit them to function legally. In addition, the government continued to prevent workers from forming independent unions and otherwise exercising their labor rights.

Government officials, at the direction of their superiors, committed most human rights abuses. Impunity for the perpetrators remained widespread.

Section 1. Respect for the Integrity of the Person, Including Freedom from:

a. Arbitrary Deprivation of Life and other Unlawful or Politically Motivated Killings

There were no confirmed reports that the government or its agents committed arbitrary or unlawful killings during the year.

b. Disappearance

There were no reports of politically motivated long-term disappearances during the year, although there were several reports of detained activists whose whereabouts were temporarily unknown because the government did not register these detentions. On August 1, the Cuban Commission on Human Rights and Reconciliation (CCDHRN), an independent human rights nongovernmental organization (NGO), reported human rights activist Carlos Manuel Figueroa could not be located. The NGO later reported that he was detained for five days and then placed under house arrest until August 13 for filming the detentions of members of the independent civil society group Damas de Blanco (Ladies in White).

c. Torture and Other Cruel, Inhuman, or Degrading Treatment or Punishment

The law prohibits abusive treatment of detainees and prisoners. There were reports, however, that members of the security forces intimidated and physically assaulted human rights and prodemocracy advocates, dissidents, and other detainees and prisoners during detention and imprisonment, and that they did so with impunity. Some detainees and prisoners endured physical abuse, sometimes by other inmates, with the acquiescence of guards.

There were reports of police assaulting detainees or being complicit in public harassment of and physical assaults on peaceful demonstrators (see section 2.b.).

On January 10, activists Antonio Rodiles and Ailer Gonzalez reported state security officers injected them with an unknown substance when they participated in a public march calling for the release of political prisoners. Medical evaluations in Miami produced inconclusive results about the nature of the substance.

On March 27, police officers allegedly beat two members of the Damas de Blanco with cables, and one Dama suffered an arm sprain. Members of the Damas de Blanco reported receiving head injuries, bites, bruises, and other injuries during government-sponsored counter protests and detentions.

On July 20, Guillermo "Coco" Farinas, president of the United Anti-Totalitarian Forum (FANTU), complained of a beating by police officers that caused injuries to his ribs, abdomen, and tongue when he tried to visit a police station to check on a fellow FANTU activist.

Prison and Detention Center Conditions

Prison conditions continued to be harsh. Prisons were overcrowded, and facilities, sanitation, and medical care were deficient. There were reports of prison officials assaulting prisoners.

Physical Conditions: The government provided no information regarding the number, location, or capacity of detention centers, which included not only prisons but also work camps and other kinds of detention facilities.

Prison and detention cells reportedly lacked adequate water, sanitation, space, light, ventilation, and temperature control. Although the government provided basic food and some medical care, many prisoners relied on family for food and other basic supplies. Potable water was often unavailable. Prison cells were overcrowded. Prisoners often slept on concrete bunks without a mattress, with some reports of more than one person sharing a narrow bunk. Where available, mattresses were thin and often infested with vermin and insects. Women also reported lack of access to feminine hygiene products and inadequate prenatal care.

Prisoners, family members, and NGOs reported inadequate health care, which led to or aggravated multiple maladies. Prisoners also reported outbreaks of dengue, tuberculosis, hepatitis, and cholera. There were reports of prison deaths from heart attacks, asthma, HIV/AIDS, and other chronic medical conditions, as well as from suicide.

Political prisoners and the general prison population were held in similar conditions. Political prisoners who refused to wear standard prison uniforms were denied certain privileges, such as access to prison libraries and standard reductions in the severity of their sentence (for example, being transferred from a maximum-security to a medium-security prison). Political prisoners also reported that fellow inmates, who they believed were acting on orders of prison authorities, threatened or harassed them.

Prisoners reported that solitary confinement was a common punishment for misconduct and that some prisoners were isolated for months at a time.

The government subjected prisoners who criticized the government or engaged in hunger strikes and other forms of protest to extended solitary confinement, assaults, restrictions on family visits, and denial of medical care.

Administration: There was no publicly available information about prison administration or recordkeeping.

A legal department within the Attorney General's Office is empowered to investigate allegations of abuse in the prison system. The results of these investigations were not publicly accessible. By law prisoners and detainees may seek redress regarding prison conditions and procedural violations, such as continued incarceration after a prison sentence has expired. Prisoners reported that government officials refused to allow or accept complaints, or failed to respond to complaints.

Prisoners and pretrial detainees had access to visitors, although some political prisoners' relatives reported that prison officials arbitrarily canceled scheduled visits. Some prisoners were able to communicate information about their living conditions through telephone calls to human rights observers and family members.

The Cuban Council of Churches, the largest Protestant religious organization, reported that it organized weekly chaplain services for all prisons in the country. There were isolated reports that prison authorities did not inform inmates of their right to access religious services, delayed months before responding to such requests, and limited visits by religious groups to a maximum of two or three times per year.

Independent Monitoring: The government did not permit monitoring of prison conditions by independent international or domestic human rights groups and did not permit access to detainees by international humanitarian organizations. Although the government pledged in previous years to allow a visit by the UN special rapporteur on torture and other cruel, inhuman, and degrading treatment or punishment, no visit occurred during the year. The government allowed foreign journalists to tour specific prisons, but others have been off-limits since 2013.

d. Arbitrary Arrest or Detention

Arbitrary arrests and short-term detentions continued to be a common government method for controlling independent public expression and political activity. By law police have wide discretion to stop and question citizens, request identification, and carry out arrests and searches. Police used laws against public disorder, contempt, lack of respect, aggression, and failing to pay minimal or arbitrary fines as ways to detain civil society activists. Police officials routinely conducted short-term detentions, at times assaulting detainees. The law provides that police officials furnish suspects a signed "act of detention," noting the basis, date, and location of any detention in a police facility and a registry of personal items seized during a police search, but this law was not always followed. Arbitrary stops and searches were most common in urban areas and at government-controlled checkpoints at the entrances to provinces and municipalities.

Police and security officials continued to use short-term and sometimes violent detentions to prevent independent political activity or free assembly. Such detentions generally lasted from several hours to several days. The CCDHRN counted 9,940 detentions through the end of the year, compared with 8,616 in 2015. Members of the #TodosMarchamos campaign, which included Damas de Blanco, reported weekly detentions of members to prevent demonstrations. The largest opposition group, Patriotic Union of Cuba (UNPACU), also reported an increase in short-term detentions. Long-term imprisonment of peaceful government critics, while rare, sometimes occurred. In December UNPACU published a list of 46 political prisoners throughout the country serving more than one month in prison for reported peaceful protests or assemblies.

The law allows a maximum four-year preventive detention of individuals not charged with an actual crime, with a subjective determination of "potential dangerousness," defined as the "special proclivity of a person to commit crimes, demonstrated by conduct in manifest contradiction of socialist norms." Mostly used as a tool to control "antisocial" behaviors, such as substance abuse or prostitution, authorities also used such detention to silence peaceful political opponents. On March 14, authorities charged UNPACU activist Luis Bello Gonzalez with precriminal social dangerousness and sentenced him to three years in prison. UNPACU leaders alleged authorities arrested and charged Gonzalez because of his regular participation in protests alongside other UNPACU members.

Role of the Police and Security Apparatus

The Ministry of Interior exercises control over police, internal security forces, and the prison system. The ministry's National Revolutionary Police is the primary law enforcement organization. Specialized units of the ministry's state security branch are responsible for monitoring, infiltrating, and suppressing independent political activity. The police supported state security agents by carrying out house searches, arresting persons of interest to the ministry, and providing interrogation facilities.

The police routinely violated procedural laws with impunity and at times failed or refused to provide citizens with legally required documentation, particularly during arbitrary detentions and searches. Security force members also committed civil rights and human rights abuses with impunity.

Although the law on criminal procedure prohibits the use of coercion during investigative interrogations, police and security forces at times relied on aggressive and physically abusive tactics, threats, and harassment during questioning. Detainees reported that officers intimidated them with threats of long-term detention, loss of child custody rights, denial of permission to depart the country, and other punishments.

There were no official mechanisms readily available to investigate government abuses.

Undercover police and Ministry of Interior agents were often present and directed activities to disrupt efforts at peaceful assembly (see section 2.b.).

According to independent reports, state-orchestrated counter protests directed against independent civil society groups and individuals, including the Damas de Blanco and other organizations, were organized to prevent meetings or to shame participants publicly (see section 2.a.). The Damas de Blanco and other members of the #TodosMarchamos campaign experienced weekly government-sponsored counter protests at their usual gathering place in Havana from January until March, when the government shut down the demonstrations altogether. Government-sponsored counter protests continued for several months outside of the Damas de Blanco headquarters to prevent large demonstrations by activists.

Arrest Procedures and Treatment of Detainees

Under criminal procedures, police have 24 hours after an arrest to present a criminal complaint to an investigative police official. The investigative police have 72 hours to investigate and prepare a report for the prosecutor, who in turn has 72 hours to recommend to the appropriate court whether to open a criminal investigation.

Within the 168-hour detention period, detainees must be informed of the basis for the arrest and criminal investigation and have access to legal representation. Those charged may be released on bail, placed in home detention, or held in continued investigative detention. Once the accused has an attorney, the defense has five days to respond to the prosecution's charges, after which a court date usually is set. Prosecutors may demand summary trials "in extraordinary circumstances" and in cases involving crimes against state security.

There were reports that defendants met with their attorneys for the first time only minutes before their trials and were not informed of the basis for their arrest within the required 168-hour period.

Reports suggested bail was available, although typically not granted to those arrested for political activities. Time in detention before trial counted toward time served, if convicted.

Detainees may be interrogated at any time during detention and have no right to request the presence of counsel during interrogation. Detainees have the right to remain silent, but officials do not have a legal obligation to inform them of that right.

By law investigators must complete criminal investigations within 60 days. Prosecutors may grant investigators two 60-day extensions upon request, for a total of 180 days of investigative time. The supervising court may waive this deadline in "extraordinary circumstances" and upon special request by the prosecutor. In that instance no additional legal requirement exists to complete an investigation and file criminal charges, and authorities may detain a person without charge indefinitely.

Arbitrary Arrest: Officials often disregarded legal procedures governing arrest, detaining suspects longer than 168 hours without informing them of the nature of the arrest or affording them legal counsel.

Pretrial Detention: The government held detainees for months or years in investigative detention, in both political and nonpolitical cases. In nonpolitical cases delays were often due to bureaucratic inefficiencies and a lack of checks on police.

<u>Detainee's Ability to Challenge Lawfulness of Detention before a Court</u>:
Detainees are able to challenge in court the legal basis or arbitrary nature of their detention, but these challenges were rarely successful, especially regarding detentions alleged to have been politically motivated. On December 6, the mother of graffiti artist Danilo Maldonado, known as "El Sexto," petitioned the court for a writ of habeas corpus after authorities detained her son on November 26; El Sexto had painted graffiti on an exterior wall of a Havana hotel. The court denied the petition, and his mother submitted a second petition on December 13, which remained pending at year's end.

e. Denial of Fair Public Trial

While the constitution recognizes the independence of the judiciary, the judiciary is directly subordinate to the National Assembly and the CP, which may remove or appoint judges at any time. Political considerations thoroughly dominated the judiciary, and there was virtually no separation of powers between the judicial system, the CP, and the Council of State.

Civilian courts exist at the municipal, provincial, and national levels. Special tribunals convene behind closed doors for political ("counterrevolutionary") cases and other cases deemed "sensitive to state security." Officials denied entry to trials by some observers during the year. Military tribunals may also have jurisdiction over civilians if any of the defendants are members of the military, police force, or other law enforcement agency.

Trial Procedures

Due process rights apply equally to all citizens as well as foreigners, but courts regularly failed to protect or observe these rights. The law presumes defendants to be innocent until proven guilty, but authorities often ignored this, placing the burden on defendants to prove innocence.

Defendants generally have the right to a public trial, but politically motivated trials were at times held in secret, with authorities citing exceptions for crimes involving "state security" or "extraordinary circumstances." Many cases were concluded quickly and were closed to the press. Interpretation was sometimes provided during trials, but the government claimed that limited resources prevented interpreters from always being available.

The law requires that defendants be represented by an attorney, at public expense, if necessary. Defendants' attorneys may cross-examine government witnesses and present witnesses and evidence. Only state attorneys are licensed to practice in criminal courts.

Criteria for admitting evidence were arbitrary and discriminatory. According to reports, prosecutors routinely introduced irrelevant or unreliable evidence to prove intent or testimony about the revolutionary credentials of a defendant.

Defense attorneys have the right to review the investigation files of a defendant, but not if the charges involve "crimes against the security of the state." In these cases defense attorneys were not allowed access until charges were filed. Many detainees, especially political detainees, reported their attorneys had difficulties accessing case files due to administrative obstacles.

In trials where defendants are charged with "potential dangerousness" (see section 1.d.), the state must show only that the defendant has "proclivity" for crime, so an actual criminal act need not have occurred. Penalties may be up to four years in prison. Authorities normally applied this provision to prostitutes, alcoholics, young persons who refused to report to work centers; repeat offenders of laws restricting change of domicile; and political activists who participated in public protests.

The law recognizes the right of appeal in municipal courts but limits it in provincial courts to cases involving lengthy prison terms or the death penalty.

Political Prisoners and Detainees

The government continued to deny holding any political prisoners but refused access to its prisons and detention centers by international humanitarian organizations and the United Nations.

The number of political prisoners was difficult to determine. Lack of governmental transparency and systemic violations of due process rights obfuscated the true nature of criminal charges, investigations, and prosecutions, allowing government authorities to prosecute and sentence peaceful human rights activists for criminal violations or "dangerousness." The government used the designation of "counterrevolutionary" for inmates deemed to be political opposition, but it did not release those numbers. The government continued to deny access to its prisons and detentions centers by independent monitors who could help determine the size of the political prisoner population. At least two independent organizations estimated there were 75 to 95 political prisoners. The government closely monitored these organizations, which often faced harassment from state police.

On September 23, authorities arrested independent lawyer Julio Alfredo Ferrer Tamayo during a police raid on the legal aid center Cubalex (see section 1.f.). Although police released all other detained employees in less than 24 hours, Ferrer remained in detention through the end of the year. According to Cubalex, Ferrer received a suspended three-year sentence in February for allegedly falsifying documents in relation to the attempted establishment of a civil society organization in 2010, and police cited this earlier arrest as a reason for refusing his release.

Political prisoners reported the government held them in isolation for extended periods. They did not receive the same protections as other prisoners or detainees. The government also frequently denied political prisoners access to home visits, prison classes, telephone calls, and, on occasion, family visits.

Civil Judicial Procedures and Remedies

Although it is possible to seek judicial remedies through civil courts for violations of administrative determinations, independent legal experts noted that general procedural and bureaucratic inefficiencies often delayed or undermined the enforcement of administrative determinations and civil court orders. Civil courts, like all courts in the country, lacked independence and impartiality as well as effective procedural guarantees. No courts allowed claimants to bring lawsuits seeking remedies for human rights violations.

f. Arbitrary or Unlawful Interference with Privacy, Family, Home, or Correspondence

The constitution protects citizens' privacy rights in their homes and correspondence, and police must have a warrant signed by a prosecutor or magistrate before entering or conducting a search. Nevertheless, there were reports that government officials routinely and systematically monitored correspondence and communications between citizens, tracked their movements, and entered homes without legal authority and with impunity. Additionally, in August civil society organizations complained that text messages containing specific words including "democracy" and "dissident" were systematically blocked.

Police searched homes and seized personal goods without legally required documentation.

In May, and again in November, UNPACU reported major search and seizure operations at private homes used as headquarters in Santiago de Cuba and Havana. In both cases police confiscated printed materials, cameras, computers, printers, flash drives, and money.

On September 23, the Center for Legal Information (Cubalex), an independent legal aid center, reported a large search and seizure operation of its headquarters. Police seized five computers, four laptops, multiple hard drives, USB drives, cell phones, and more than 300 records of legal cases. Police also strip-searched Cubalex lawyers, threatened the employees with prison time, and opened an investigation into their alleged illicit activities.

The Ministry of Interior employed a system of informants and neighborhood committees, known as "Committees for the Defense of the Revolution," to monitor government opponents and report on their activities. Agents from the ministry's General Directorate for State Security subjected foreign journalists, visiting foreign officials and diplomats, academics, and businesspersons to frequent surveillance, including electronic surveillance.

The CP is the only legally recognized political party, and the government actively suppressed attempts to form other parties (see section 3). The government encouraged mass political mobilization and favored citizens who actively participated (see section 2.b.).

Family members of government employees who leave international work missions without official permission at times faced government harassment or loss of employment, access to education, or other public benefits.

Section 2. Respect for Civil Liberties, Including:

a. Freedom of Speech and Press

The constitution provides for freedom of speech and press only insofar as it "conforms to the aims of socialist society." Laws banning criticism of government leaders and distribution of antigovernment propaganda carry penalties ranging from three months to 15 years in prison.

<u>Freedom of Speech and Expression</u>: The government had little tolerance for public criticism of government officials or programs and limited public debate of issues considered politically sensitive. State security regularly harassed the organizers of independent fora for debates on cultural and social topics to force them to stop discussing issues deemed controversial. Forum organizers reported assaults by state security, video surveillance installed outside of venues, and detention of panelists and guests on the days they were expected to appear.

Several government workers reported being fired for expressing dissenting opinions or affiliating with independent organizations. For example, in August local radio station journalist Jose Ramirez Pandoja was fired for publishing a controversial speech by the deputy director of the CP's official newspaper, *Granma,* on his personal blog. The speech cited young journalists leaving traditional media outlets due to censorship policies and low salaries.

Several university professors and researchers reported they were forced from their positions or demoted for expressing ideas or opinions outside of government-accepted norms.

During the year some religious groups reported greater latitude to express their opinions during sermons and at religious gatherings, although most members of the clergy continued to exercise self-censorship. Religious leaders in some cases criticized the government, its policies, and even the country's leadership without reprisals. The Roman Catholic Church operated a cultural and educational center in Havana that hosted debates featuring participants expressing different opinions about the country's future. On January 8, the government closed open-air churches in Camaguey and Las Tunas and detained three pastors associated with the Apostolic movement, an unregistered network of Protestant churches. The government claimed that the pastors erected the churches without permission, but the pastors denied that claim. One of the pastors was later charged and convicted of violating neighborhood noise ordinances related to his Sunday sermons.

<u>Press and Media Freedoms</u>: The government directly owned all print and broadcast media outlets and all widely available sources of information. News and information programming was generally uniform across all outlets, with the exception of broadcasts of Venezuelan government news programming. The government also controlled nearly all publications and printing presses, and the CP must give prior approval for printing of nearly all publications. The party censored public screenings and performances. The government also limited the importation of printed materials. Foreign correspondents in the country had limited access to

and often were denied interviews with government officials. They also struggled to gather facts and reliable data for stories. Despite meeting government vetting requirements, official journalists who reported on sensitive subjects did so at personal risk, and the government restricted the ability of official journalists to work for unofficial media outlets in addition to their official duties. *Granma* correspondent Jose Antonio Torres remained in prison at the end of the year; he was sentenced in 2012 to 14 years' imprisonment on charges of espionage for articles he wrote.

Violence and Harassment: The government does not recognize independent journalism, and independent journalists sometimes faced government harassment, including detention and physical abuse. Most detentions involved independent journalists who filmed arrests and harassment of #TodosMarchamos activists. Several journalists were detained, had their equipment confiscated, and were harassed for covering the aftermath of Hurricane Matthew. Some independent journalists reported interrogations by state security agents for publishing articles critical of government institutions.

Censorship or Content Restrictions: The law prohibits distribution of printed materials considered "counterrevolutionary" or critical of the government. Foreign newspapers or magazines were generally unavailable outside of tourist areas. Distribution of material with political content--interpreted broadly to include the Universal Declaration of Human Rights, foreign newspapers, and independent information on public health--was not allowed and could result in harassment and detention.

The government sometimes barred independent libraries from receiving materials from abroad and seized materials donated by foreign governments, religious organizations, and individuals. Government officials also confiscated or destroyed cameras and phones of individuals to prevent them from distributing photographs and videos deemed objectionable, such as those taken during arrests and detentions. Activists reported interrogations and confiscations at the airport when arriving from the United States. On August 1, human rights activist Ivan Hernandez Carillo reported being detained and beaten when he arrived at the airport in Havana after he refused to go to a small room to have his belongings searched. On August 12, independent lawyer Laritza Diversent was briefly questioned when she returned from testifying on freedom of expression before the UN special rapporteur. Security officials confiscated all materials related to this event. Independent think tank Convivencia reported nine police citations and interrogations in September and October during which state security questioned members about their participation in international conferences.

Libel/Slander Laws: The government uses defamation of character laws to arrest or detain individuals critical of the country's leadership.

Internet Freedom

The government restricted or disrupted access to the internet and censored some online content, and there were credible reports that the government monitored without appropriate legal authority the limited e-mail and internet chat rooms and browsing that were permitted. The government controlled all internet access, except for limited facilities provided by a few diplomatic missions and a small but increasing number of black market facilities.

While the International Telecommunication Union reported that 31 percent of citizens used the internet in 2015, access often was limited to a national intranet that offered only e-mail or highly restricted access to the World Wide Web. Other international groups reported lower internet penetration, with approximately 5 percent of the population having access to open internet.

The government selectively granted internet access to certain areas in the city and sectors of the population consisting mostly of government officials, established professionals, some professors and students, journalists, and artists. Others could access e-mail and internet services through government-sponsored "youth clubs," internet cafes, or Wi-Fi hot spots approved and regulated by the Ministry for Information, Technology, and Communications. Users were required to purchase prepaid cards and provide personal information in order to access the internet in these centers.

During the year the government increased the number of Wi-Fi hot spots at computer centers to more than 200 countrywide. The government also expanded Wi-Fi hot spots in areas outside computer centers and proposed a pilot program to install internet in the homes of a limited number of persons in Old Havana. Authorities reviewed the browsing history of users, reviewed and censored e-mail, employed internet search filters, and blocked access to websites considered objectionable. Access cost approximately two convertible pesos (CUC) ($2) per hour, still beyond the means of many citizens, whose average official income was approximately 23 CUC ($23) per month.

While the law does not set specific penalties for unauthorized internet use, it is illegal to own a satellite dish that would provide uncensored internet access. The government restricted the importation of wireless routers, reportedly actively targeted private wireless access points, and confiscated equipment.

The use of encryption software and transfer of encrypted files are also illegal. Despite poor access, harassment, and infrastructure challenges, a growing number of citizens maintained blogs in which they posted opinions critical of the government, with help from foreign supporters who often built and maintained the blog sites. The government blocked local access to many of these blogs. In addition, a small but growing number of citizens could use Twitter, Facebook, Instagram, and other social media channels to report independently on developments in the country, including observations critical of the government. Like other government critics, bloggers faced government harassment, including detention and physical abuse.

Foreigners could buy internet access cards from the national telecommunications provider and use hotel business centers, where internet access could be purchased only in hard currency. Access usually cost between five and 10 CUC ($5 to $10) an hour, a rate well beyond the means of most citizens. Citizens usually could purchase internet access at the national telecommunications provider and use hotel business centers.

Human rights activists reported frequent government monitoring and disruption of cell phone and landline services prior to planned events or key anniversaries related to human rights. The government-owned telecommunications provider ETECSA often disconnected service for human rights organizers, often just before their detention by state security, or to disrupt planned activities.

During the 54-day hunger strike of activist Guillermo "Coco" Farinas, the government reportedly disrupted Farinas' telephone service and intercepted calls to provide false information.

Academic Freedom and Cultural Events

The government restricted academic freedom and controlled the curricula at all schools and universities, emphasizing the importance of reinforcing "revolutionary ideology" and "discipline." Some academics refrained from meeting with foreigners, including diplomats, journalists, and visiting scholars, without prior government approval and, at times, the presence of a government monitor. Those permitted to travel abroad were aware that their actions, if deemed politically unfavorable, could negatively affect them and their relatives back home. During the year the government allowed some religious educational centers greater space to operate.

Outspoken artists and academics faced some harassment and criticism orchestrated by the government. For example, in April academic Omar Everleny Perez Villanueva was expelled from the Center for the Study of the Cuban Economy at the University of Havana for "indiscipline" and for having "unauthorized conversations with foreign institutions," which included talking to foreign press and criticizing the government's slow pace of economic reforms.

In June art historian Yanelys Nunez Leyva was fired from a cultural magazine for contributing to a developing online platform called the Cuban Museum of Dissent featuring leaders in Cuban history who had rebelled against political doctrines.

Public libraries required citizens to complete a registration process before the government granted access to books or information. Citizens could be denied access if they could not demonstrate a need to visit a particular library. Libraries required a letter of permission from an employer or academic institution for access to censored, sensitive, or rare books and materials. Religious institutions organized small libraries. Independent libraries remained illegal but continued to exist and faced harassment and intimidation.

b. Freedom of Peaceful Assembly and Association

Freedom of Assembly

Although the constitution grants a limited right of assembly, the right is subject to the requirement that it may not be "exercised against the existence and objectives of the socialist state." The law requires citizens to request authorization for organized meetings of three or more persons, and failure to do so could carry a penalty of up to three months in prison and a fine. The government tolerated some gatherings, and many religious groups reported the ability to gather without registering or facing sanctions.

Independent activists faced greater obstacles, and state security forces often suppressed attempts to assemble, even for gatherings in private dwellings and in small numbers. This trend was particularly pronounced in the eastern part of the country. For example, on March 27, UNPACU reported that state security forces forcibly detained more than 150 activists in the provinces of Santiago de Cuba, Las Tunas, and Guantanamo during a peaceful protest.

The government also continued to organize repudiation acts in the form of mobs organized to assault and disperse those who assembled peacefully. Participants arrived in government-owned buses or were recruited by government officials from nearby workplaces or schools. Participants arrived and departed in shifts, chanted revolutionary slogans, sang revolutionary songs, and verbally taunted the targets of the protest. The targets of this harassment at times suffered physical assault or property damage. Government security officials at the scene, often present in overwhelming numbers, did not arrest those who physically attacked the victims or respond to victims' complaints and instead frequently orchestrated the activities. Officials reportedly took direct part in physical assaults.

The government did not grant permission to independent demonstrators or approve public meetings by human rights groups or others critical of any government activity.

In July police began blocking private UNPACU meetings in eastern provinces. On September 22, police detained 24 activists who were attempting to participate in a routine UNPACU meeting. Separately, in Havana, on September 22, police detained three labor union activists and placed five under house arrest to stop a meeting organized by human rights activist Ivan Hernandez Carrillo. The government also blocked meetings for independent academic and cultural organizations. For example, on September 23, Dagoberto Valdes, founder and director of the think tank Convivencia, suspended a course in Pinar del Rio on civic learning after two civil society participants from Cienfuegos were barred from entering the province.

Freedom of Association

The government routinely denied citizens freedom of association and did not recognize independent associations. The constitution proscribes any political organization not officially recognized. A number of independent organizations, including opposition political parties and professional associations, operated as NGOs without legal recognition.

Recognized churches (including the Roman Catholic humanitarian organization Caritas), the Freemason movement, and a number of fraternal and professional organizations were the only associations legally permitted to function outside the formal structure of the state, the CP, and government-organized groups. Religious groups are under the supervision of the CP's Office of Religious Affairs, which has the authority to deny permits for religious activities and exerted pressure on church leaders to refrain from including political topics in their sermons.

Nonreligious groups must register through the Ministry of Justice to receive official recognition. Authorities continued to ignore applications for legal recognition from new groups, including several new religious groups as well as women's rights and gay rights organizations, thereby subjecting members to potential charges of illegal association.

The government continued to afford preferential treatment to those who took an active part in CP activities and mass demonstrations in support of the government, especially when awarding valued public benefits, such as admissions to higher education, fellowships, and job opportunities.

c. Freedom of Religion

See the Department of State's *International Religious Freedom Report* at www.state.gov/religiousfreedomreport/.

d. Freedom of Movement, Internally Displaced Persons, Protection of Refugees, and Stateless Persons

There continued to be restrictions on freedom of movement within the country, foreign travel, and migration with the right of return. The government also controlled internal migration from rural areas to Havana.

In-country Movement: Although the constitution allows all citizens to travel anywhere within the country, changes of residence to Havana were restricted. The local housing commission and provincial government authorities must authorize any change of residence. The government may fine persons living in a location without authorization from these bodies and send them back to their legally authorized place of residence. There were reports that authorities limited social services to persons who lived in Havana illegally. Police occasionally threatened to prosecute for "dangerousness" anyone who returned to Havana after expulsion.

The law permits authorities to bar an individual from a certain area within the country, or to restrict an individual to a certain area, for a maximum of 10 years. Under this provision authorities may internally exile any person whose presence in a given location is determined to be "socially dangerous." Some dissidents reported that authorities prevented them from leaving their home provinces or detained and returned them to their homes.

Foreign Travel: The government continued to require several classes of citizens to obtain permission for emigrant travel, including highly specialized medical personnel; military or security personnel; many government officials, including academics; and some former political prisoners or well-known activists. In December 2015 the government reimposed exit permit requirements on medical personnel for nonimmigrant travel, reversing a 2012 law that simplified the process by only requiring a supervisor's permission. In March the government allowed former political prisoners arrested during the 2003 Black Spring--and released in 2010 and 2011 on parole--one opportunity to travel outside the country for the first time since their arrest. Government authorities barred a second attempt when two of these activists requested permission to travel in July.

Emigration and Repatriation: Individuals seeking to migrate legally stated they also faced police interrogation, fines, harassment, and intimidation, including involuntary dismissal from employment. Government employees who applied to migrate legally to the United States reportedly sometimes lost positions when their plans became known. Some family members of former government employees who emigrated from the island lost public benefits or were denied passports to travel and join their family members abroad.

The law provides for imprisonment of up to three years or a fine of 500 nonconvertible pesos (CUP) ($20) for first-time "rafters" (those who attempted to depart using clandestinely constructed vessels). The largest fine reported during the year was 3,000 CUP ($120) for an unauthorized departure from the country. Most persons caught attempting unauthorized departures via sea were detained briefly. In the case of military or police defectors, or those traveling with children, the punishment could be more severe. Prison terms were also more common for persons attempting to flee to the United States through the Guantanamo U.S. Naval Station.

Under the terms of the 1994 U.S.-Cuba Migration Accord, the government agreed not to prosecute or retaliate against migrants returned from international or U.S. waters, or from the U.S. Naval Station at Guantanamo, after attempting to emigrate illegally if they had not committed a separate criminal offense. The government prevented independent trips to monitor repatriated Cubans outside of Havana.

Some would-be migrants alleged harassment and discrimination, such as fines, expulsion from school, and job loss, and others reported more severe punishment.

Protection of Refugees

Access to Asylum: The constitution provides for the granting of asylum to individuals persecuted for their ideals or actions involving a number of specified political grounds. The government has no formal mechanism to process asylum for foreign nationals.

Temporary Protection: On the small number of cases of persons seeking asylum, the government worked with the Office of the UN High Commissioner for Refugees and other humanitarian organizations to provide protection and assistance, pending third-country resettlement. In addition, the government allowed foreign students who feared persecution in their home countries to remain in the country after the end of their studies, until their claims could be substantiated or resolved.

Section 3. Freedom to Participate in the Political Process

While a voting process to choose candidates exists, citizens do not have the ability to choose their government through the right to vote in free and fair elections or run as candidates from outside the CP, and the government retaliated against those who sought peaceful political change.

Elections and Political Participation

Recent Elections: Government-run bodies prescreened all candidates in the April 2015 municipal elections, and once approved by the CP, candidates ran for office mostly uncontested. There were reports that the government altered the public biographies of non-CP candidates who attempted to run in the elections by labeling them as "counterrevolutionaries."

Political Parties and Political Participation: Government-run commissions preapproved all CP candidates for office and rejected independent candidacies without explanation or the right of appeal. Dissident candidates reported the government tampered with their candidate biographies and organized protests to besmirch their names. The government routinely used propaganda campaigns in the state-owned media to criticize its opponents.

Participation of Women and Minorities: There were no official restrictions on women or minorities, and the government actively promoted participation of both in government. According to *Granma*, women constituted 30 percent of the Council of Ministers, 39 percent of the Council of State, 49 percent of the National Assembly, and more than half of the provincial presidents. Women remained underrepresented in the most powerful decision-making bodies; there were no women on the executive committee of the Council of Ministers, or in positions of military leadership.

Section 4. Corruption and Lack of Transparency in Government

The law provides criminal penalties for corruption, and the government was highly sensitive to corruption allegations and often conducted anticorruption crackdowns.

Corruption: The law provides for three to eight years' imprisonment for "illegal enrichment" by authorities or government employees. The government did not implement the law effectively, and officials sometimes engaged in corrupt practices with impunity. There were numerous reports of law enforcement and other official corruption in enforcement of a myriad of economic restrictions and government services. There were widespread reports of police corruption. Multiple sources reported that when searching homes and vehicles, police sometimes took the owner's belongings or sought bribes in place of fines or arrests.

Financial Disclosure: The law does not require appointed and elected officials to disclose their assets.

Public Access to Information: The law provides for public access to government information, but requests for information routinely were rejected. The government engaged in limited public outreach activities.

Section 5. Governmental Attitude Regarding International and Nongovernmental Investigation of Alleged Violations of Human Rights

The government did not recognize domestic human rights groups or permit them to function legally. Several human rights organizations continued to function outside the law, including the CCDHRN, UNPACU, the Christian Liberation Movement, the Assembly to Promote Civil Society, and the Lawton Foundation for Human Rights. The government subjected domestic human rights advocates to intimidation, harassment, and periodic short-term detention.

No officially recognized, independent NGOs monitored human rights. The government refused to recognize or meet with any unauthorized NGOs that monitored human rights. Furthermore, there were reports of explicit government harassment of individuals who met with unauthorized NGOs.

<u>The United Nations or Other International Bodies</u>: The government continued to deny international human rights organizations, the United Nations and its affiliate organizations, and the International Committee of the Red Cross access to prisoners and detainees.

<u>Government Human Rights Bodies</u>: For the first time, the Cuban government hosted a structured bilateral dialogue in which Cuban authorities provided substantive comments about human rights problems in the country.

Section 6. Discrimination, Societal Abuses, and Trafficking in Persons

Women

<u>Rape and Domestic Violence</u>: The law criminalizes rape, including spousal rape, and the government enforced the law. Penalties for rape are at least four years' imprisonment, with longer prison terms or death as possible penalties, depending on the circumstances of the rape.

The law does not recognize domestic violence as a distinct category of violence but prohibits threats and violence, including those associated with domestic violence. Penalties for domestic violence are covered by provisions against assault and range from fines to prison sentences of varying lengths, depending on the severity of the offense.

To raise awareness about domestic violence, the government continued to carry out media campaigns. Official television, radio, and print media occasionally discussed issues pertaining to women, including domestic violence. In addition, a few government-organized groups held conferences and worked with local communities to improve services. The UN Children's Fund (UNICEF) reported that the government ran counseling centers for women and children in most municipalities, with staff trained in assisting victims of abuse.

<u>Sexual Harassment</u>: The law provides penalties for sexual harassment, with potential prison sentences of three months to five years. The government did not

release any statistics on arrests, prosecutions, or convictions for offenses related to sexual harassment during the year. Civil society groups noted sexual harassment was underreported.

Reproductive Rights: Couples and individuals have the right to decide the number, spacing, and timing of their children; manage their reproductive health; and have access to the information and means to do so, free from discrimination, coercion, and violence. Access to information on modern contraception and skilled health attendance during pregnancy, at delivery, and in postpartum care was available, but access to information and contraception to prevent the spread of HIV/AIDS was limited.

Discrimination: The law accords women and men equal rights, the same legal status, and the same responsibilities with regard to marriage/divorce, parental duties, home maintenance, and professional careers. The law grants working mothers preferential access to goods and services and provides for equal pay for equal work.

Children

Birth Registration: Citizenship is normally derived by birth within the country's territory, and births were generally registered promptly. Those who emigrate abroad and have children must request a Cuban passport for the child before re-entering Cuba. Children born outside of Cuba to parents on official business are granted Cuban citizenship.

Child Abuse: There was no apparent pattern of violence against or abuse of children. The government operated 174 guidance centers for women and families, charged with providing family counseling services and other assistance to individuals harmed by intrafamilial violence.

Early and Forced Marriage: The legal minimum age of consent for marriage is 18. Marriage for girls as young as 14 and for boys as young as 16 is permitted with parental consent. According to UNICEF, 40 percent of women ages 20-24 were married before age 18, and 9 percent of women ages 20-24 were married before 15. There was no available information on the government's efforts to prevent or mitigate early marriage.

Sexual Exploitation of Children: Prostitution is legal for those age 16 and older. While there were numerous reports of underage prostitution, there were no reliable statistics available regarding its extent. In October 2015 the government reported that 2,122 children were victims of sexual abuse in 2014. The minimum age of consent is 16. There is no statutory rape law, although penalties for rape increase as the age of the victim decreases. The law imposes seven to 15 years' imprisonment for involving minors under 16 in pornographic acts. The punishment may increase to 20 to 30 years or death under aggravating circumstances. The proposal to participate in such acts is punishable with two to five years' imprisonment. The law does not criminalize the possession of pornography, but it punishes the production or circulation of any kind of obscene graphic material with three months' to one year's imprisonment and a fine. The offer, provision, or sale of obscene or pornographic material to minors under 16 is punishable with two to five years in prison. International trafficking of minors is punishable with seven to 15 years' imprisonment.

The government maintained centers in Havana, Santiago de Cuba, and Santa Clara for the treatment of child sexual abuse victims. The centers employed some modern treatment techniques, including the preparation of children to be witnesses in criminal prosecutions.

International Child Abductions: The country is not a party to the 1980 Hague Convention on the Civil Aspects of Child Abduction. See the Department of States *Annual Report on International Parental Child Abduction* at travel.state.gov/content/childabduction/en/elgal/compliance.html.

Anti-Semitism

There were between 1,000 and 1,500 members of the Jewish community. There were no reports of anti-Semitic acts.

Trafficking in Persons

See the Department of State's *Trafficking in Persons Report* at www.state.gov/j/tip/rls/tiprpt/.

Persons with Disabilities

No known law prohibits discrimination against persons with disabilities in employment, education, access to health care, or the provision of other state services. The Ministry of Labor and Social Security is in charge of the Employment Program for Persons with Disabilities. A ministry resolution accords persons with disabilities the right to equal employment opportunities and equal pay for equal work. No information was available on compliance with this resolution. The law recommends that buildings, communication facilities, air travel, and other transportation services accommodate persons with disabilities, but these facilities and services were rarely accessible to persons with disabilities, and information for persons with disabilities was limited.

The Special Education Division of the Ministry of Education is responsible for the education and training of children with disabilities. Children with disabilities attended school; no information was available on whether there were patterns of discriminatory abuse in educational facilities or in mental health facilities during the year. Some religious organizations reported they were permitted to help provide educational programs for children with disabilities.

National/Racial/Ethnic Minorities

Although the government's declared policy favors racial integration and inclusiveness, Afro-Cubans often suffered racial discrimination, including disproportionate stops for identity checks and searches, and some were subject to racial epithets while undergoing unlawful beatings at the hands of security agents in response to political activity. Afro-Cubans also reported employment discrimination, particularly in sought-after positions within the tourism industry and at high levels within the government. Afro-Cubans were represented disproportionately in neighborhoods with the worst housing conditions and were economically disadvantaged.

Acts of Violence, Discrimination, and Other Abuses Based on Sexual Orientation and Gender Identity

The law prohibits discrimination based on sexual orientation in employment, housing, statelessness, or access to education or health care. Nonetheless, societal discrimination based on sexual orientation or gender identity persisted.

Mariela Castro, President Castro's daughter, headed the National Center for Sexual Education and continued to be outspoken in promoting the rights of lesbian, gay, bisexual, transgender, and intersex (LGBTI) persons. Throughout the year the government promoted the rights of LGBTI persons, including nonviolence and nondiscrimination in regional and international fora. In May the government sponsored a march and an extensive program of events to commemorate the International Day Against Homophobia and Transphobia.

Several unrecognized NGOs promoted LGBTI issues and faced some government criticism, not for their promotion of such topics, but for their independence from official government institutions. In June several independent organizations attempted to organize an LGBTI march in Havana to celebrate LGBTI Pride Month. According to independent reports, authorities detained several activists to prevent their participation in the march and reportedly asked others not to leave their homes that day, limiting participation to fewer than five activists.

HIV and AIDS Social Stigma

There were reports that some persons with HIV/AIDS suffered job discrimination. The government operated four prisons exclusively for inmates with HIV/AIDS; some inmates were serving sentences for "propagating an epidemic." Special diets and medications for HIV patients were routinely unavailable.

Section 7. Worker Rights

a. Freedom of Association and the Right to Collective Bargaining

The law, including related regulations and statutes, severely restricts worker rights by recognizing only the CP-controlled Workers' Central Union of Cuba (CTC) as the paramount trade union confederation. All trade groups must belong to the CTC to operate legally. The law does not provide for the right to strike. The law also does not provide for collective bargaining, instead setting up a complicated process for reaching collective agreements. The International Labor Organization continued to raise concerns regarding the trade union monopoly of the CTC, the prohibition on the right to strike, and restrictions to collective bargaining and agreements, including that government authorities and CTC officials have the final say on all such agreements.

The government continued to prevent the formation of independent trade unions in all sectors. The CP chose the CTC's leaders. The CTC's principal responsibility is to manage government relations with the workforce. The CTC does not bargain collectively, promote worker rights, or advocate for the right to strike. The CTC led information dissemination regarding the government's planned large-scale layoffs of government workers and in defending the government's decision to do so.

Several small, independent labor organizations operated without legal recognition, including the National Independent Workers' Confederation of Cuba, the National Independent Laborer Confederation of Cuba, and the Unitarian Council of Workers of Cuba; together they comprise the Independent Trade Union Association of Cuba, which was created in October to replace the Coalition of Independent Unions of Cuba. These organizations worked to advance the rights of workers by offering an alternative to the state-sponsored CTC, and by advocating for the rights of small business owners and employees who represent 29 percent of the country's labor force. The independent unions were reportedly harassed by police and infiltrated by government agents, limiting their capacity to represent workers effectively or work on their behalf.

The government may determine that a worker is "unfit" to work, resulting in job loss and the denial of job opportunities. Persons were deemed unfit because of their political beliefs, including their refusal to join the official union, and for trying to depart the country illegally. The government also penalized professionals who expressed interest in emigrating by limiting job opportunities or firing them.

b. Prohibition of Forced or Compulsory Labor

The law does not appear to prohibit forced labor explicitly. It prohibits unlawful imprisonment, coercion, and extortion, with penalties ranging from fines to imprisonment, but there was no evidence that these provisions were used to prosecute forced labor cases. The use of minors in forced labor, drug trafficking, prostitution, pornography, or organ trade is punishable by seven to 15 years' incarceration.

Compulsory military service of young men was occasionally fulfilled by assignment to an economic entity controlled by the military or by assignment to other government services. Allegations of forced or coerced labor in foreign medical missions persisted, although the government denied these allegations.

The government continued to use some high school students in rural areas to harvest agricultural products (also see section 7.c.).

Also see the Department of State's *Trafficking in Persons Report* at www.state.gov/j/tip/rls/tiprpt/.

c. Prohibition of Child Labor and Minimum Age for Employment

The legal minimum working age is 17, although the law permits the employment of children ages 15 and 16 to obtain training or fill labor shortages with parental permission and a special authorization from the municipal labor director. The law does not permit children ages 15 and 16 to work more than seven hours per day or 40 hours per week or on holidays. Children ages 15 to 18 cannot work in specified hazardous occupations, such as mining, or at night.

There were no known government programs to prevent child labor or remove children from such labor. Antitruancy programs, however, aimed to keep children in school. Inspections and penalties appeared adequate to enforce the law, as inspections for child labor were included in all other regular labor inspections. The government reported more than 700 such inspections of state-run and private-sector enterprises during 2015. The government penalizes unlawful child labor with fines and suspension of work permits. There were no credible reports that children under the age of 17 worked in significant numbers.

The government used some high school students in rural areas to harvest agricultural products for government cooperatives during peak harvest time. Student participants were not paid but received school credit and favorable recommendations towards university admission. Failure to participate or obtain an excused absence reportedly could result in unfavorable grades or university recommendations, although students were reportedly able to participate in other activities (instead of the harvest) to support their application for university admission. There were no reports of abusive or dangerous working conditions.

d. Discrimination with Respect to Employment and Occupation

The law prohibits workplace discrimination based on skin color, gender, religious belief, sexual orientation, nationality, "or any other distinction harmful to human dignity," but it does not explicitly protect political opinion, social origin, disability, age, language, gender identity, or HIV-positive status or other communicable diseases. No information was available on government enforcement of these provisions during the year.

Discrimination in employment and occupation occurred with respect to persons with HIV and members of the Afro-Cuban population. Leaders within the Afro-Cuban community noted that some Afro-Cubans could not get jobs in sectors such as tourism and hospitality because they were "too dark." Afro-Cuban leaders explained that fairer-skinned citizens filled jobs in sectors that deal with tourists, and these jobs were often among the best-paying positions available. Afro-Cubans more frequently obtained lower-paying jobs, including cleaning and garbage disposal, which prevented them from interacting with tourists, a major source of hard currency.

There were no statistics stating whether the government effectively enforced applicable laws.

e. Acceptable Conditions of Work

The monthly minimum wage was fixed at 225 CUP ($9). The minimum wage requirement does not apply to the non-state sector, including the self-employed. The government supplemented the minimum wage with free education, subsidized medical care (daily wages are reduced by 40 percent after the third day of a hospital stay), housing, and some food. Even with subsidies, the government acknowledged that the average wage of 600 CUP ($24) per month did not provide a reasonable standard of living.

The standard workweek is 44 hours, with shorter workweeks in hazardous occupations, such as mining. The law provides workers with a weekly minimum 24-hour rest period and 24 days of paid annual holidays. These standards apply to state workers as well as to the non-state sector, but not to the self-employed. The law does not provide for premium pay for overtime or prohibit obligatory overtime, but it generally caps the number of overtime hours at 12 hours per week, or 160 per year. The law provides little grounds for a worker to refuse to work overtime. Refusal to work overtime can result in a notation in the employee's official work history that could imperil subsequent requests for vacation time. The Ministry of Labor has the authority to establish different overtime caps as needed. Compensation for overtime is paid in cash at the regular hourly rate or in additional rest time, particularly for workers directly linked to production or services, and it does not apply to management. Workers complained that overtime compensation was either not paid or not paid in a timely manner.

The government set workplace safety standards and received technical assistance from the International Labor Organization to implement them. The Ministry of Labor enforced the minimum wage and hours-of-work standards through offices at the national, provincial, and municipal levels, but the government lacked mechanisms to adequately enforce occupational safety and health standards. There was no information available about the number of labor inspectors. Reports from recent years suggested there were very few inspectors and that health and safety standards frequently were ignored or subject to corrupt practices.

According to government statistics, 518,479 workers were self-employed during the year, an increase of 5 percent from 2015; the total workforce in the private sector increased from approximately 25 percent to 29 percent. Self-employed and private-sector workers obtained licenses by applying to the Ministry of Labor and were subject to inspection by the government. The government maintained a list of 201 trades that may be plied privately and allowed the self-employed to hire labor. Despite criminal penalties for doing so, a significant number of workers participated in the informal economy, including individuals who actively traded on the black market and those performing professional activities not officially permitted by the government. There were no reliable reports or statistics about the informal economy.

Foreign companies operated in a limited number of sectors, such as hotels, tourism, and mining. Such companies operated on the basis of a joint venture in which the government contracted and paid company workers in pesos an amount that was a small fraction of what the company remitted to the state for labor costs. Most formal employment took place only through government employment agencies. Employers, including international businesses and organizations, were generally prohibited from contracting or paying workers directly, although many reportedly made supplemental payments under the table. The Ministry of Labor enforces labor laws on any business, organization, or foreign governmental agency based in the country, including wholly owned foreign companies operating in the country, joint-stock companies involving foreign investors operating in the country, the United Nations, international NGOs, and embassies. Cuban workers employed by these entities are subject to a number of labor regulations common to most state and non-state workers, together with some regulations specific for these kinds of entities. Government bodies, including the tax collecting agency, the Ministry of Finance and Prices, enforced regulations. There were no reports about protections for migrant workers' rights.

Past reports from an independent union cited some violations of health and safety standards at worksites throughout the country, including inadequate and poorly maintained equipment and protective gear. Official government reports cited 3,432 workplace accidents in 2015 (a reduction of 357 compared with 2014) and 70 workplace deaths (the same as 2014). The CTC provided limited information to workers about their rights and at times did not respond to or assist workers who complained about hazardous workplace conditions. It was generally understood that workers could not remove themselves from dangerous situations without jeopardizing their employment, and authorities did not effectively protect workers facing this dilemma.